Allyship

&

Me

A SELF-PACED PERSONAL GROWTH PLAYBOOK & JOURNAL

FOR COMPASSIONATE HUMANS WHO VALUE EQUITY & INCLUSION

Embrace Anti-Racism | Use Your Privilege for Good |
Help Create a More Equitable World

Copyright © 2021 Talisa Lavarry

All rights reserved. This book or any portion thereof may not be reproduced or used in any manner whatsoever without the express written permission of the publisher except for the use of brief quotations in a book review.

Printed by Yum Yum Morale, LLC, in the United States of America

First printing, 2021.

Yum Yum Morale, LLC
2226 Eastlake Ave. E. #26
Seattle, WA 98102

https://yumyummorale.com

Dedication

This workbook is dedicated to those who have entered my life within the last two years having no hidden agendas or motivations outside of lending a hand. While I've been bruised and broken as a result of my race and gender, I also know what true allyship looks and feels like. I'm hesitant to name names because I know that I can't possibly list everyone. You know who you are.

To My Allies,
Cheers!

TABLE OF CONTENTS

Dear Aspiring Ally,	5
Welcome to your personal authentic allyship journey!	7
What Is Allyship, Exactly?	8
Part 1:	9
Authentic Allyship Is a Journey, Not a Destination	9
Take Off Your Cape and Slow Down	12
How to Proceed without Overstepping	14
Understanding Privilege	14
A Moment of Reflection	17
This Work Is Time-Consuming—Pace Yourself!	18
Your Role	20
Consider:	22
Chart Your Path	26
How We Got Here	28
Prejudice	28
Discrimination	30
Racism	31
Systemic Racism	33
The Role of White-Centering in Systemic Racism	39
Consider this:	47
Part 2:	53
Arm Yourself with Knowledge and Humility	53
A Quick History	56
Authentic Knowledge, Authentic Action	62
Casey's Next Steps	63
Overcoming White Fragility with Humility	67
Where the Rubber Meets the Road	74
Responsibility	74
Think about it:	75
The Work	77
Consider:	79
Part 3:	83
Adopt Your Personal Allyship Plan	83
The conversation:	90
ACKNOWLEDGEMENTS	93
Resources	94

Dear Aspiring Ally,

When I decided to write my book, Confessions From Your Token Black Colleague, I never imagined that I'd receive so many requests for a second one. Countless times I've responded with a resounding NO, followed by chuckles.

I can imagine that drafting, writing, and publishing anything can be challenging. Going through the emotions of past lived experiences can be even more laborious. However, here I am just over a year later, releasing yet another labor of love.

For the past two years, I've started and managed my workplace diversity, equity, and inclusion consultancy. It has been one of the most challenging, yet rewarding experiences of my life. One of my favorite parts of the experience is the time I've spent with clients who reach out to me for anti-racism coaching. The foundation of my coaching program is two-pronged: the first being systemic racism, the second being allyship.

In Fall 2021, TedX Seattle Women invited me to become a part of the prestigious roster of speakers. With gratitude, I accepted the call. I knew that I wanted to use the opportunity to share what I believed to be the most profound message that my clients were picking up. Ultimately, in the midst of all of the lectures and trainings offered, the question I would hear over and over again was, "How can I be a part of the solution?" While my answer would vary some, it would always end with the understanding that allyship was the key.

This playbook and journal is the perfect compliment to my TedXTalk, coaching sessions, and curriculum offered through my consultancy, Yum Yum Morale LLC. It is also great on its own.

No matter the capacity in which I work with clients, I make it clear that my goal isn't to help them achieve perfection or completion. My goal is to be a very instrumental part of their journey.

Creating this playbook and journal allows me another opportunity to touch more people in yet another way.

I am beyond excited to present this work to you, and appreciate your trust in me. As you work through this book you may have some specific questions, epiphanies, and thoughts. Always feel free to reach out directly. It sincerely warms my heart to hear from you.

Cheers!
Tali

True Allyship is Opening Doors that the Marginalized Can't Open for Themselves.

-- Talisa Lavarry

Welcome to your personal authentic allyship journey!

Congratulations on making the decision to come alongside people of color as an ally. It's a courageous decision that will have a lasting impact on those around you and those who choose to continue the fight towards justice after you. Your transition from bystander to ally will cause you some discomfort, but the payout will be a better, fairer, and more accepting environment for all of us who find our home here in the United States of America, regardless of our origins and identities.

My goal is to serve as your personal guide on your allyship journey as you unlearn what you've likely believed your whole life, replace false narratives with real, diverse ones, and take bold actions, whether people see them or not. Parts of this transition will be hard, however, hard things are not impossible. Join me as I lead you towards necessary contextual background and practices to help you embrace anti-racism, use your privilege for good, and shape a more equitable world.

In this workbook we will:

1. Look at authentic allyship as a journey, not a destination,
2. Recenter the importance and power of knowledge, and
3. Build and adapt your personal allyship plan.

Now that you're ready to get started, this journal will assist you in creating a personalized allyship plan and journey. If you do this with pure intentions, I'm sure your actions will have a positive impact in your life and the world. This kind of commitment is the very thing that creates the change so many of us work toward every day.

What Is Allyship, Exactly?

Over the past few years, many words connected to our changing social climate have made their way into our lexicons, some of which aren't easy to define. Take a moment to consider what allyship means to you. Write your definition in the blanks below.

Part 1:

Authentic Allyship Is a Journey, Not a Destination

Our society portrays certain demographics as standard. Anyone apart from the standard is often considered an outlier, and outliers usually do not enjoy the same level of basic human rights promised to us all. A person who recognizes this and wants to do something about it is called an "ally", therefore, *allyship is the practice of seeking to ensure the same rights for all of us, a practice which often includes social justice.*

Before you can grow, you need to know your baseline. Now that you know the definition of an ally, take 60 seconds to record characteristics of allies, actions allies should take, and any other words that reflect someone in the role. This activity serves as a starting point which you will use later to measure your personal growth, so don't think too hard or search elsewhere for answers. Set your timer for one minute and go for it.

Allyship

Characteristics of Allies	Actions of Allies	Words that describe Allies

Allies are courageous individuals who understand the importance of action. They don't whisper their opposition to the status quo and cross their fingers in hopes of future change. Allyship requires effort towards anti-racism and anti-oppression work. Ideally, you would implement this work in every facet of your life, but oftentimes, you may not even recognize your blind spots towards the daily realities of those you seek to align with. That's why this transition must be thorough and approached from a place of humility.

I know, I know—this might sound overwhelming right now, but understand that the indoctrination of our country being "the greatest country of all time" essentially begins at birth. Your belief system, molded by school, religious organizations, media, and even loved ones, has likely been shaped by both overtly and covertly racist attitudes, words, and actions that created these blind spots.

By becoming an ally, you've committed to rooting out the problematic belief that everyone has access to the same opportunities and replacing it with an inclusive mindset that recognizes inequities and injustices. This could mean anything from a notable adjustment to a complete overhaul of what you've always believed about the country you love and the people who helped shape your thinking.

Facing My Biases

Complete the faces below based on your feelings about the biased nature of the USA.

| Yesterday | Today | Tomorrow |

Yesterday, I felt: _____

Today, I feel: _____

Tomorrow, I hope to feel: _____

Sometimes, the passion of the task at hand can overtake sensibilities. When that happens, many would-be excellent allies fall into the trap of doing too much too fast for their own personal benefit. We call these people "white saviors." Take a moment to jot down your definition of this term:

_____

Take Off Your Cape and Slow Down

White saviors are white people who seek to help non-whites from an attitude of self-service. All too often, they care more about speed than impact. This speed isn't coming from a place of urgency for a better today, but rather a personal need to erase their own guilt and shame. This is NOT the way to achieve allyship. Instead, you need to focus your efforts in a slow and steady way. Let's explore an example of the white savior.

Johnny puts in a lot of work in the last ungentrified block of his gentrified city, painting a wall tarnished by graffiti. He is working and sweating, sweating and working, posting photos on social media for all to see how good a person he is. His chest inflates with pride until he is informed, after all his toiling, that the wall he's painted is a sacred space for elders and children who live on that block to display their art.

When speeding towards quick fixes overcomes listening, engaging, and planning, allyship can become irresponsible and dangerous. Slow down. A problem that took centuries to nurture cannot be fixed overnight.

White Saviors R Us

The characters pictured below have been accused of performative advocacy. Create a quick story about what they did.

Next, let's look at an example of true allyship. Meet Ben.

Ben is the manager at the store where Ashlee works. Ashlee is an excellent employee who goes out of her way to serve her customers well. One day, a couple comes into the store looking for a product that has been discontinued. When Ashlee tells them they don't carry the product anymore, the couple accuses her of being too lazy to look for it. They then proceed to complain to Ben who, in turn, asks the couple to leave the store. Ben later assures Ashlee that he sees the work she does each day, he appreciates her, and the company's diversity statement isn't just for optics.

When you choose to be an ally, understand that you are in it for the long haul. It is not enough to be nice, show up for one march, or back out when you get tired. Justice and advancement for marginalized people are slow, and you can't hurry the process along at the pace you so choose or throw in the towel when times get too tough. If you are ready to take on the lifelong burden of ensuring "liberty and justice for all" so all of us may be judged by the content of our character instead of the color of our skin, then let's get to the real work.

How to Proceed without Overstepping

To be a good ally, knowing what not to do is just as important as knowing what to do. The excitement and fervor of social justice movements can open our eyes to things we've never seen before, but they can also propel us to places that aren't beneficial. When stepping in as an ally, remember to give earnest effort without looking for the spotlight. Be careful not to stand in front of or speak for those seeking equality. Your role is supportive in nature; those you are supporting can speak for themselves.

Understanding Privilege

When you choose allyship, it's because you recognize the privilege that comes with living as a member of the dominant demographic. Before we go any further, let's establish this foundational truth: _There is nothing wrong with privilege._

Notice how you feel when you hear the word "privilege". Does it elicit frustration from you? Does it make you feel ashamed? The truth is most of us carry privilege in one capacity or another; what matters is what we choose to do with it.

In the table below, you're going to make two lists. In the first column, list characteristics, achievements, beliefs, or other aspects of yourself that compel others to extend privilege to you. In the second column, list those aspects of yourself that compel others to marginalize or oppress you. You have 30 seconds per column.

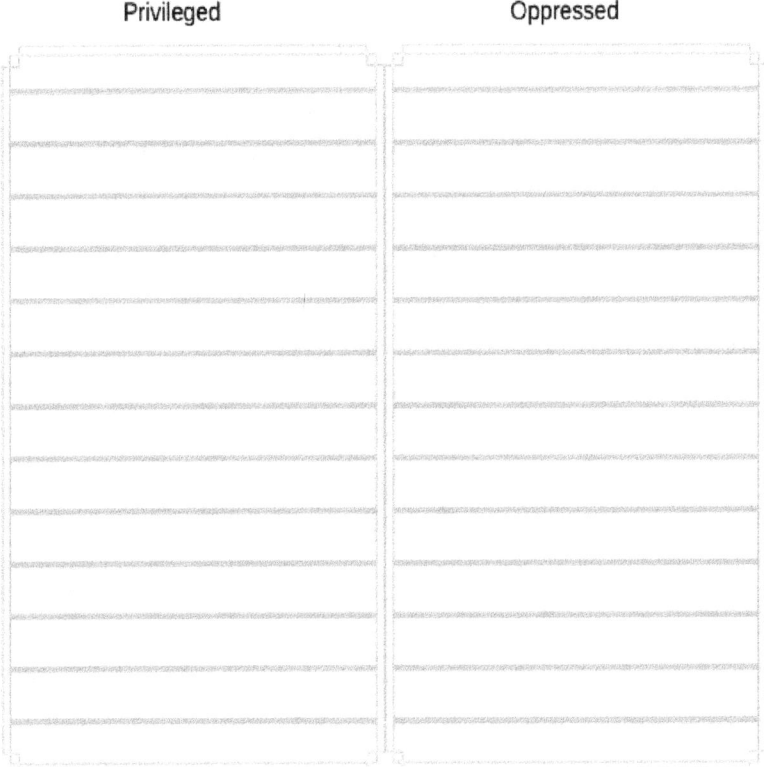

Understanding my Privilege

Privileged	Oppressed

You are working through this book because you've made the decision to use your privilege to improve humanity, and that is a selfless act that should make you proud. As an advocate, it's important to remember your motives. Before you go out to do the work, whether it be to sit in on a town hall or march in a protest, ask yourself:

- Am I doing this for social media likes?   Yes   No
- Am I doing this so people can praise me?   Yes   No
- Am I doing this from a place of purity, even if I gain no recognition at all?   Yes   No

Your honest answers to these questions will help you maintain the right perspective. But if, in fact, you are participating for likes and praise, you are engaging in what's called "performative allyship".

Performative allyship comes from a place of *me*, not a place of *us*. It's easy to spot, especially when difficult events take place or conversations get messy, as they often do when attempting to wade through and untangle the roots of systemic injustice.

The truth is you may hold ideals that are racist or otherwise prejudiced in nature without even knowing it, and you know what? That's okay, as long as you're willing to address these mindsets and work to deconstruct them when they arise.

Even more than marching, that's what the heart of allyship is all about.

A Moment of Reflection

Now that we've described performative allyship, can you recall a time when you engaged in this way or overstepped without realizing it? Briefly describe the incident, then follow it with what you would have done differently had you known then what you know now.

_____
_____
_____
_____
_____
_____
_____
_____
_____
_____
_____
_____
_____
_____
_____
_____
_____
_____
_____
_____
_____
_____
_____
_____
_____

Take responsibility for the ways you've contributed to injustice in the past, then move forward. No one is asking you to wallow in guilt; that serves no purpose. Instead, keep learning, keep interacting, keep listening, and keep acting from a pure heart that magnifies the faces and voices of those who have been silenced all too long.

This Work Is Time-Consuming—Pace Yourself!

Allyship is about authenticity. Look over your common practices and consider old habits you can replace with new ones. Support BIPOC-owned businesses when you can, become a better listener and observer of marginalized people's realities, and consistently evaluate your own thinking and interactions with others. These practices will help mold you into a co-conspirator in the fight for justice.

This journey is an up, down, back, and forth process that requires constant deconstruction and reconstruction to be sustainable.

To change the world, we must begin with <u>ourselves</u>.

Are you ready? Of course you are!

"We all have a sphere of influence. Each of us needs to find our courage so that others can begin to speak."

--Beverly Daniel Tatum

Your Role

Beverly Tatum, award-winning thought leader, best-selling author, and expert on the psychology of racism, is right—courage is the key. The more we use it, the stronger it becomes. We can build courage through large and small acts, both of which are noble and can move us closer to our goal.

Consider your own unique personality, experiences, gifts, and talents. What skillsets or personality traits do you possess that can help propel the movement forward? Are you a graphic artist? Teacher? Yoga instructor? Consider designing graphics for events or websites pointed towards the cause, influencing syllabi in your school to include literature by BIPOC artists or studies of BIPOC scientists, or offering meditations to community leaders.

In the spaces below, make a list of the skills, traits, talents, and experiences you can utilize when engaging in acts of allyship.

Defining me

Skills   Traits

When combined with a heart for positive change, your skills are invaluable. Don't be shy—use what you have so we can all get what we want.

Consider:

1. What prominent issues are facing your country, state, and city right now that you would like to see change most?

___

2. On a 10-point scale, how mentally and emotionally equipped do you feel to make change towards these challenges?

Unequipped   Fully Equipped

3. How have you contributed your skills and expertise in the past in ways that yielded positive results? What ongoing efforts stemmed from those contributions?

_____
_____
_____
_____
_____
_____
_____
_____
_____
_____
_____
_____
_____
_____
_____
_____
_____
_____
_____
_____
_____
_____
_____
_____
_____

4. How can you offer your skills and expertise to the people around you now?

I hope you realize your value towards positive change. It is immeasurable.

The role you play as an ally is exceedingly important. Why? People in the majority have influence. Your perspective carries more weight than that of marginalized individuals because you are already viewed as being on equal footing with others in the majority.

That being said, I know it can be intimidating to stand by marginalized groups.

In my TedTalk, I offered my experience of having my hard work ignored and being told my wealth of qualifications wouldn't be able to overcome the disadvantage of my race as I climbed the corporate ladder for two reasons:

1. So listeners could see the impact of oppression, and
2. By hearing how my colleagues stepped in, listeners could know it is possible to be an effective ally.

Going down this road can cost you socially, emotionally, and even financially. However, the legacy you'll leave behind will hopefully be everlasting, so don't lose sight of the gains, no matter how small they might seem in light of what you might lose.

You're likely fired up and ready to make positive change somewhere, but remember—you can't do everything. Don't even try to. You will become overwhelmed and burn out, and that does not help anyone. Even though you can't do everything, you can do something, so while you're figuring out what that is, consider how much time you realistically have to offer and where you can be of most assistance without turning the light towards yourself.

Chart Your Path

Research organizations in your community that are working towards positive change. How can you contribute to work that's already happening?

Research the one that speaks to you the most and give them a call this week to ask if they have any immediate needs. Don't make any commitments yet; just listen. Once you hear their answers, brainstorm ways you can meet those needs.

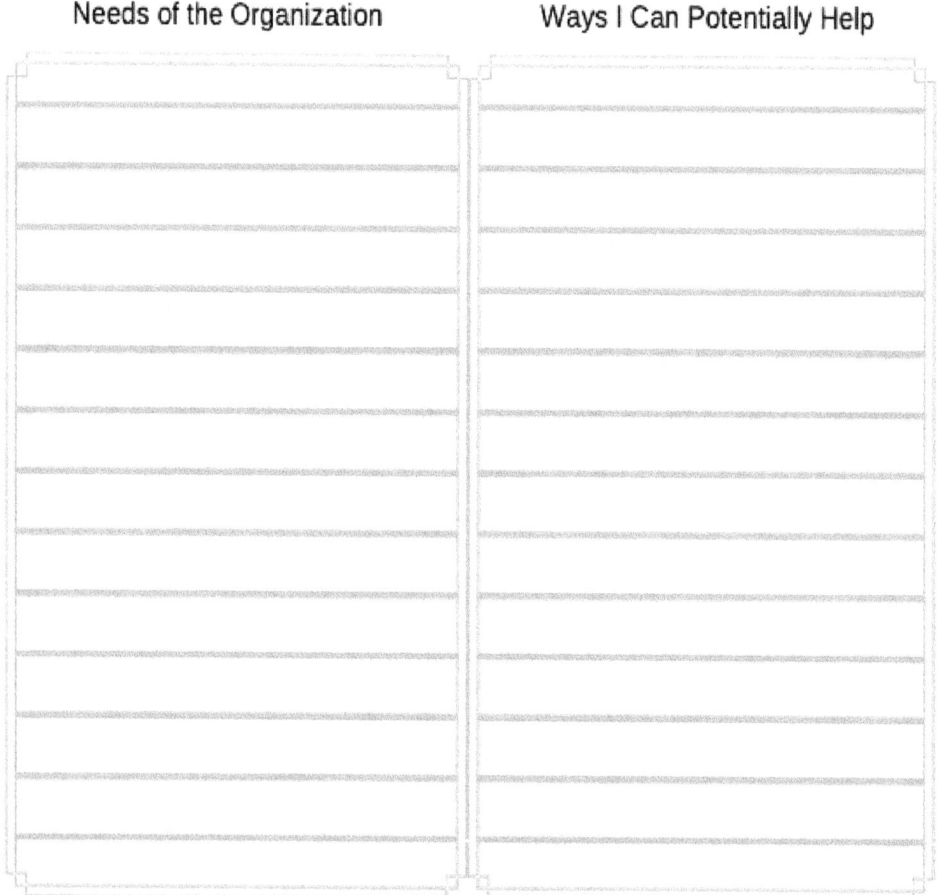

"In a racist society it is not enough to be non-racist; we must be anti-racist."

--Angela Davis

How We Got Here

Ibram X. Kendi has made "anti-racism" a household term, one with widespread implications and applications. Let's look at how racial injustice begins with prejudice and escalates to systemic racism.

Prejudice

Prejudice is a preconceived opinion that is not based on reason or actual experience.

Prejudice is like the telephone game from elementary school. Somebody says one thing. That listener relays the information to someone else, and by the time the message has made the rounds a few times, it has become severely distorted.

Prejudice is the result of low-level thinking and oversimplification. Let's think about how this shows up in our day to day lives.

Think about the last time you watched a movie. Take a moment to reflect on the diversity in the movie and each of the characters' roles. Movies and TV shows often portray certain races as the bad guys. Watch enough television that perpetuates this message, and you might begin to conclude that people of that race are inherently geared towards committing like crimes.

This is what we call conditioning, which is the lifeblood of prejudice. Once the concept of inherent evil settles into the mind, it doesn't take much to transfer thoughts from prejudice to discrimination.

Take a moment to reflect on the last thing you watched relating to this notion. Briefly write your thoughts here, then complete the activity.

Discrimination

Discrimination is "the unjust or prejudicial treatment of different categories of people, especially on the grounds of ethnicity, age, sex, or disability."[1] Of course, for the purposes of this workbook, we are focusing on ethnicity or race. Discrimination involves a power dynamic, as does every level of racial injustice from this point on. It means making a distinction between groups and adjusting behavior according to who you think deserves better or worse treatment.

There is a fine line between this concept and the next. Consider segregated schools and the idea of separate but equal. The distinction between Black and white students and the continued separation of the two was an act of discrimination. Thinking white students deserved better resources was an act of discrimination. Providing better resources to white students was crossing the line from discrimination to racism. During that time, people would say, "All men are created equal, it's just that some are more equal than others," and who got to decide who was "more equal"?

The powers that were, who then controlled the messaging from various media to influence the public to believe the same. This ability to control resources, messaging, and the outcome of people's lives based on race is racism.

What immediately comes to mind when you read this?

_____
_____
_____
_____
_____
_____
_____
_____
_____
_____
_____
_____
_____
_____
_____

---

[1] "Discrimination." https://www.lexico.com/en/definition/discrimination

Racism

Racism is "a belief or doctrine that inherent differences among racial groups determine cultural or individual achievement."[2] Racism is carried out by a group who believes they are superior. Notice the distinction: racism has to be carried out by those in power. Racism removes all individuality or opportunity for nuance within personalities and lifestyles, puts everyone in their specific color box, and treats them according to however those in power so choose.

Historically, the founders of our country deemed Black people subhuman and only granted rights and privileges in full to those on the opposite end of the spectrum. This injustice lingers today and has outlasted law changes and movements. Legislation has changed over time, but hearts and collective mindsets have moved even more slowly. That's why it's important that you are participating in this journey.

Racism in the United States is determined by a color hierarchy that affects finances, friendships, marriages, home purchases, voting rights and accessibility, and many other facets of American life. These problems exist because they have been written into the system. That brings us to the problem we're attempting to eradicate: systemic racism.

---

[2] "Racism." https://www.dictionary.com/browse/racism

"A lie doesn't become truth, wrong doesn't become right, and evil doesn't become good, just because it's accepted by the majority."

--Booker T. Washington

Systemic Racism

NAACP President Derrick Johnson defines systemic racism as, "systems and structures [of] procedures or processes that disadvantage African Americans."[3] In the United States, since we have citizens of many races, we see racism play out in a hierarchical format.

Since the country's inception, the white race has deemed itself superior and created laws and systems to keep them in that position. Likewise, the white race deemed the Black race inferior and created laws and systems to keep us in that position, as well. Through concerted efforts in government, education, and even entertainment, the belief that the white race is superior and the Black race falls at the bottom of the hierarchy has been adopted by the collective American psyche. This mindset is pervasive to the point where non-white ethnicities are willing to adopt views that demean themselves and others in an effort to acquire white approval and privilege.

Such a shift is possible because of the spread of misinformation about Black people (prejudice) and the sources of this information that we are taught to count as credible. This control of information and perspective is what we call "white supremacy", or supreme control over a narrative and protection from the consequences of unjust actions.

Systemic racism refers to elements woven into a society's laws and regulations that prevent minorities from achieving, or even existing, as easily as their white counterparts. These operations not only permit discriminatory treatment from person to person, but also from the government to a demographic as a whole.

Think about Florida's "stand your ground" law[4] and the outcome of the George Zimmerman case. The law enabled the murder of Trayvon Martin, therefore, Zimmerman served no time for killing him. This set off a string of murders that were excused simply because the murderers "feared for their lives", an argument that is often employed when Black people are murdered by those in powerful positions.

---

[3]Koppelman, Andrew. https://www.usatoday.com/story/opinion/2020/09/23/systemic-racism-how-really-define-column/5845788002/
[4]"Stand Your Ground and Castle Doctrine Laws." https://billofrightsinstitute.org/e-lessons/stand-your-ground-and-castle-doctrine-laws-elesson

What are some other examples of systemic racism you see in your town, county, state, and country? Reflect on how those have impacted others and have impacted you?

_____
_____
_____
_____
_____
_____
_____
_____
_____
_____
_____
_____
_____
_____
_____
_____
_____
_____
_____
_____
_____
_____
_____
_____

The term "systemic racism" was coined in 1967 to show the differences between racism woven into the system and carried out without thought versus racism extended from one individual to another.[5] The proponents of the concept believed individual racism was easier to spot because it had a more overt nature. Discriminatory behavior is clearer in an individual than in an entire system, especially when the system doesn't use the same language as an inflamed person would. Systemic racism might even be carried out by people we trust and who we believe see things from our worldview; its ability to hide makes it more threatening. This is the very reason it has, until now, received far less collective condemnation than acts of individualized racism.

---

[5]Gonzalez, Juan Carlos.
https://go.gale.com/ps/i.do?id=GALE%7CA252849366&sid=googleScholar&v=2.1&it=r&linkaccess=abs&issn=15350584&p=AONE&sw=w&userGroupName=anon%7E2ad6102a

When people begin to see the systemic racism around them, the bravest in society speak up, but most people choose comfort, keep their heads down, and get along the best they can or deny that such behavior could ever exist in the land of opportunity. When you consider the daily grind of work, relationships, education, family difficulties, and natural disasters, how much strength do most people really have to put towards social justice?

This is one of many reasons the fight is still raging—it takes time, patience, and energy to overturn systems, and most of us simply don't have an abundance of those resources, especially if the injustice doesn't affect us.

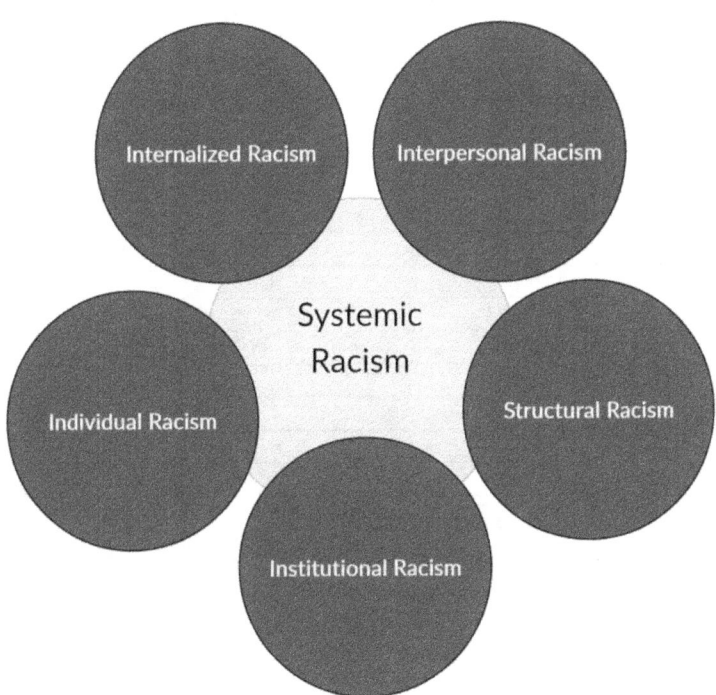

Systemic racism lasts because of the ease of replication. It seeps into every facet of society, including education, employment, housing, and healthcare. Politicians or aspiring politicians can easily uphold systemic racism in the name of gaining a voter base or retaining their positions, and those who push back often become the objects of vitriol.

Let's take some time to brainstorm specific ways we've seen systemic racism play out before our eyes.

1. List and give examples of two instances of systemic racism happening in the United States right now. If you can't think of any yourself, research them.

_____
_____
_____
_____
_____
_____
_____
_____
_____
_____
_____
_____
_____
_____
_____
_____
_____
_____
_____
_____
_____
_____
_____
_____
_____
_____
_____
_____
_____

2. For each of the instances of systemic racism you listed in the previous question, list 2-3 potential solutions.

3. What role could you personally play, using your gifts and talents, in implementing the solutions you listed in the previous question?

The Role of White-Centering in Systemic Racism

White people are not ignorant of injustice served to Black people in our country. Jane Elliot, antiracism expert, has made a practice of asking her audiences of white Americans to stand up if they would like to receive the same treatment Black Americans receive in this country, and they never stand up. She reiterates that they know there's a problem, and anybody who's honest would agree.

If you have not yet seen one of these moments, I encourage you to look at her work on YouTube and take a moment to reflect on your answer to the question.[6]

I also encourage you to think about your reaction if you were asked the same question by a Black woman or man. Consider how many resources you've used that were created by POC. White researchers and authors have taken it upon themselves to share our experiences, and their work garners more recognition, praise, and validity than POC authors. This is disheartening because the people who have actually had the experiences are often tossed aside.

Research books by POC authors and white authors that cover the same topics, then research the reach and success of each and take note of the differences.

---

[6]Foster, Alyssa. https://www.youtube.com/watch?v=xUIqTNwm-mk

Allies Read Books

Use this space to retain a list of books you come across that you believe will be helpful to your journey.

Layla F. Saad coined the term "white centering" in *Me and White Supremacy*, which she defines as "centering white people, white values, white norms and white feelings over everything and everyone else."[7] She goes on to explain how this attitude can manifest as tone policing, white fragility, white exceptionalism, or violence.

Essentially, this is the idea that the typical experience a white person has in a scenario is the singular experience for everyone, and if a person of color is having a different experience, they must be doing something wrong. If only POC would adjust their behavior, attitude, or appearance, they could also enjoy the same outcomes. You can spot this attitude in people when they push back against someone who tries to share their hurtful lived experiences with responses like, "Well, that didn't happen to *me*," or, "I didn't see/feel that when I did a, b, or c."

They don't realize that such rebuttals are only proving the point.

Knowing the POC experience is different from their own is exactly the knowledge that could make a doubter a tremendous ally, but for those who aren't ready to see the truth, what follows instead is a declaration of their lack of privilege and how they've had to struggle just like everyone else. If you've heard of "weaponized white tears", this is what it means.

While it's true that having white skin does not mean life is easy, it is equally true that the reason for hardship is not race. Lack of hardship due to race is what people refer to when they speak of privilege.

Use the following pages to map out your current thought process concerning BIPOC communities. Consider how you think members of the BIPOC community see the world and process information. Then, do the same for yourself.

---

[7] Saad, Layla F., and Robin DiAngelo. *Me and White Supremacy: Combat Racism, Change the World, and Become a Good Ancestor.* Thorndike Press, a Part of Gale, a Cengage Company, 2020.

HOW I SEE THE MINDS OF BIPOC COMMUNITIES

HOW I SHOULD SEE THE MINDS OF BIPOC COMMUNITIES

A PEEK INSIDE MY MIND

Have you ever heard of the term "weaponized white tears"? If so, please take a moment to reflect on when you were introduced to the term and how it made you feel then vs. now. If not, what are your initial thoughts about the term and how it impacts yourself and others?

_____
_____
_____
_____
_____
_____
_____
_____
_____
_____
_____
_____
_____
_____
_____
_____
_____
_____
_____
_____
_____
_____
_____
_____
_____

If you find yourself positioning your experience as the standard when people share their pain with you, you are white-centering. While white-centering may not seem dangerous, it is an extension of white supremacy.

When people hear the term "white supremacy", they often think of the KKK and formulate a picture in their heads of sheet-covered men lighting crosses on fire, or men with bare chests, shaved heads, and combat boots shouting, "White power!" However, white supremacy isn't always as outwardly sinister as that.

Attorney: Teens in KKK Garb Shocked Black Teen With Stun Gun

The attorney for a Black teenager from Texas says several other teens attacked his client with a stun gun on Halloween while wearing costumes resembling Ku Klux Klan robes.

By Associated Press

Nov. 11, 2021

Any idea or behavior that stems from the belief that white people are superior, the standard, or the authority, and are therefore the rightfully dominant group in society, is white supremacy.

Consider this:

Who writes the textbooks distributed in American classrooms? Who decides what shows air on primetime television or what songs play on the radio?

A 2020 *New York Times* story titled, "Faces of Power: 80% Are White, Even as U.S. Becomes More Diverse," states, "The most powerful people in the United States pass our laws, run Hollywood's studios and head the most prestigious universities. They own pro sports teams and determine who goes to jail and who goes to war."[8]

This visual that accompanies the article shows exactly who these faces belong to, to give the reader a clear picture of who's running the show. Seeing this, it's easy to understand why white-centering takes place and why it's easy to view white people as the standard. The idea that white people are not only in control, but they are somehow more qualified to run the show, is a core belief.

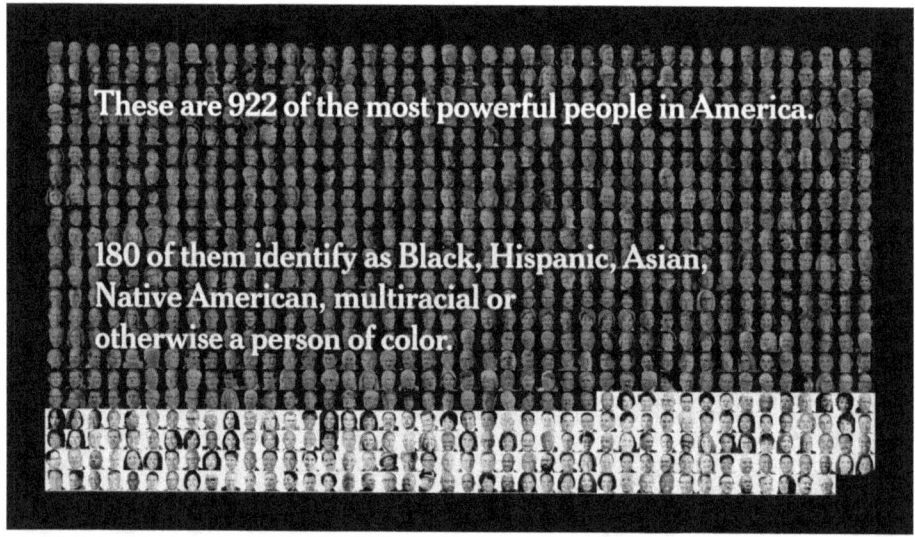

Psychology Today explains, "Core beliefs are essentially the glasses you wear which give meaning to what your senses experience in the world. [T]hey cannot be disproved because they are all encompassing. When you experience something that does not align with your core belief, your mind will immediately find a way to either disqualify it or interpret it as further validation to your core belief."[9]

---

[8] Lu, Denise, et al. https://www.nytimes.com/interactive/2020/09/09/us/powerful-people-race-us.html
[9] Romanelli, Assael, Ph.D. https://www.psychologytoday.com/us/blog/the-other-side-relationships/202001/core-beliefs-the-hammer-we-hold-in-our-hand#:~:text=These%20beliefs%20are%20called%20core%20beliefs%20and%20they,they%20cannot%20be%20disproved%20because%20they%20are%20all-encompassing.

This is called cognitive dissonance and will be a common feeling during your allyship journey. Reflect on this. How are you feeling now? How are you planning on adjusting to new information?

_____
_____
_____
_____
_____
_____
_____
_____
_____
_____
_____
_____
_____
_____
_____
_____
_____
_____
_____

Spend a few minutes thinking through concepts we've discussed in the workbook that caused cognitive dissonance for you. Record those concepts and your reactions here.

Cognitive Dissonance

Although so much of what we know comes from people we love, we must remain strong in separating the whitewashed truth from reality. It's hard to believe those trustworthy people would steer us wrong, but remember, they learned what they know from those before them. The good news is you can end the cycle.

Remember when I said being an ally can cost you? When you become vocal about going against the grain, you might lose positions, friends, or even family. You must determine what truth is worth to you; otherwise, it will become easy to shrink back when the going gets tough. Now is a good moment to release your feelings through the art of journaling. Journaling is a discipline, a strategy that helps us put things in perspective. If you just think about a concept, you might forget ideas that need to stick. Journaling solidifies our thoughts and gives us the opportunity to return to them.

By now, you're probably feeling heaviness in your chest. Sit with that feeling for a while and work through it. Take a moment to journal what you feel right now and why.

_____
_____
_____
_____
_____
_____
_____
_____
_____
_____
_____
_____
_____
_____
_____
_____
_____
_____
_____
_____
_____
_____
_____
_____

Seeing yourself: A self-portrait exercise

part 1:

1. Take a selfie with a camera. Look at the photo for 1 minute.
2. Set a timer for five minutes.
3. Draw your self-portrait from memory until the timer rings.

part 2:

1. Set the timer for 3 minutes.
2. Flip the paper and look at your first drawing.
3. Draw the upside-down image and stop when the timer rings.

Compare both drawings with the original photo.
How are they similar and different from each other?
Which one is closer to the photo you took?
What was easier to draw?

Part 2:

Arm Yourself with Knowledge and Humility

To effectively do the work of allyship, you must have a working understanding of the historical context behind the system we're living in today.

If you don't know the root causes and lived experiences that have resulted from the systems at play, it is almost impossible to know how to defeat them. The human psyche assumes everyone is living life with the same foundations and challenges we are; it takes empathy to understand how far from the truth that notion really is.

Take a moment to reflect on how two or three historical events concerning race relations stand out to you. After that, do some research on the topics and note something new you learned about the events.

Moment in history	New information

My Ultimate Coping Playlist

We go through different positive and negative emotions everyday. It is okay to have all those feelings but we must also find ways to cope.

Fill each box with the title of songs (and their artist) that you think fit the descriptions provided.

FOR AMUSEMENT

a song that gets stuck in my head

a song I know all the words to

a song from my favorite movie or tv series

TO UPLIFT

a song I associate to freedom

a song that gives me energy

a song I'd like to wake me up

FOR DIVERSION

a song that makes me feel safe

a song that helps me think positively

a song that inspires me

TO DISCHARGE

a song for when you get anxious or worried

a song for when you get angry or annoyed

a song for when you feel lonely or afraid

FOR STRONG EMOTIONS

a song that reminds you of a good memory

a song that makes you think of a loved one

a song to remind you that you are loved

A Quick History

Conversations about race are hard. They make people uncomfortable, and while people might be willing to work towards equity, there seems to be no universal end to the issue of racism. Racism is always someone's fault, but people don't want to talk about it because they don't want to feel like it's *their* fault. Even though the proof and history of the dangers of racism are readily available and still in our faces, when it comes to doing something about it, many people take the easy way out and deny there's a problem at all. However, if we keep that mindset, we'll keep getting the same results.

When you hear that racism is always someone's fault, what comes to mind?

Are you ready for some uncomfortable truths? Racism was invented by powerful white people. Let me give you a quick history:

According to Howard Zinn's *A People's History of the United States*, the colonial elite was growing more fearful of the unity of the groups they'd marginalized. In chapter three, Zinn writes, "Even before there were so many blacks, in the seventeenth century, there was, as Abbot Smith puts it, 'a lively fear that servants would join with Negroes or Indians to overcome the small numbers of masters.'" After expounding on Bacon's Rebellion of 1676, the first rebellion to unite black and white indentured servants with enslaved Black people against the government, Zinn goes on to explain that in the 1720s, there was more fear of rebellion, so white Virginian servants were allowed to join the militia, whereas before, only white freedmen could do so.

Simultaneously, the Virginian government established what they called slave patrols, which were mostly comprised of poor white men, who, by capturing those who had escaped, would receive monetary rewards. "Racism was becoming more and more practical," says Zinn, and the colonists threw gas on the idea by issuing a little power to the powerless who looked like them to ensure and sustain their own power.

Zinn quotes Edmund Morgan, "If freemen with disappointed hopes should make common cause with slaves of desperate hope, the results might be worse than anything Bacon had done. The answer to the problem, obvious if unspoken and only gradually recognized, was racism, to separate dangerous free whites from dangerous black slaves by a screen of racial contempt."[10]

Now you know how the idea was sewn into the American fabric. How has racism been sustained over the years? Power structures. Take a moment and map out some major moments in history that show power structure over time.

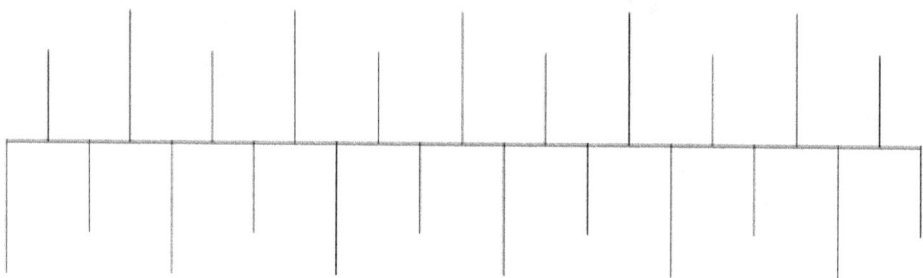

When you benefit from the power structure, as horrid as its history might be, you probably don't want to let go of those benefits. Anyone who is willing to be honest understands the formation of the America we know today was murderous and vile, and anybody who's willing to see what's happening in front of them will admit that it still is.

---

[10] Zinn, Howard. *A People's History of the United States.* Harper, 2017.

Where people get stuck is thinking they have to feel guilty and take offense for our recognition of the work of their likely ancestors. If you don't like the way things are, don't get offended that people who look like you made them that way—do what you can to change them. Energy people spend denying privilege and claiming bootstrap-pulling is the way to success is the energy they could be spending changing the way our country operates. But you know that, and that's why you are doing the work to be an effective ally.

Knowing history—real history—not only gives insight into the mindsets that created today's society, but also how people have chipped away at it bit by bit, leading to the collective loss of power and opportunity that are part of the Black experience.

"What's the matter? It's the same distance!"

Although we have seen a recent spike in interest in our country's true history, we still have a long way to go. When you learn about the historic and systemic obstacles that have been strategically placed in marginalized communities, you also learn how much further along marginalized people would be had it not been for those obstacles. This is important to consider when thinking critically about why lawmakers make the decisions they do. To understand the plight of marginalized communities, learn of their experiences from their vantage points.

Take a moment to think about those in power in your state. What do they look like? What are their values? The platform they ran on? How long have they held their position? How old are they (important to understanding generational ideology differences)? Who usually runs against them?

___

You must reconstruct truth outside of this country's standard education system because you cannot learn about activism in the same place you learned to cause harm.

The textbooks and speeches that taught you problematic patterns will never tell you the truth. Utilize the vast educational platforms before you, and get ready to get uncomfortable. The ability to see your country with all its shortcomings is a radical move, although it comes with the risk of being called unpatriotic and un-American. However, there's nothing more inherently American than pushing for liberty and justice for all.

Once we grasp this, anti-racism only makes sense.

Amazing Things I've Learned About People of Color

Use this space to write, draw, or glue photos of amazing things about people of color.

Authentic Knowledge, Authentic Action

You might be wondering the best way to go about reconstructing your mindset about treatment of marginalized people in the USA. Let's look at an example. Meet Casey.

Casey is an aspiring ally who proudly posted the list of her favorite books by Black authors on her fridge. She's learned the lingo of allyship, watched the shows that explore racism in America, and even moved some funds into a Black-owned bank. These things have their place and are a good start, but if she wants to be truly authentic, she needs to go deeper.

Is she paying attention to the everyday lives of marginalized people? Is she exploring how they are different from her in conjunction with the characteristics, hopes, and dreams they share? Does she look at their humanity with dignity instead of guilt or sorrow? What are their cares and concerns? Where are they thriving? Where could they use some assistance?

Make a list of practical next steps Casey can take to go deeper in her understanding of marginalized groups.

Casey's Next Steps

Allyship means getting in the trenches with those you seek to serve and immersing yourself in their world while still being yourself and asking questions that will help increase your understanding. This is your time to switch positions. Remember, your willingness to be the minority, and perhaps the least aware person in the room, will be the greatest teacher in antiracism and authentic allyship that you could ever experience.

If it stings to admit people who look like you committed such atrocities against those with darker skin tones, well, that's a human response. But consider this: the Quakers, who were also white, were avid abolitionists. Take on their energy instead, and fight the good fight. Your skin tone doesn't determine your character. Recognize that some people, both Black and white, will be against you no matter what. If you know you are doing the right thing, their feelings towards you aren't your responsibility.

All you can do is your best, and only you can know what that is.

Take 10 seconds to look at the word search below and highlight the first three words you see.

A	H	K	S	C	A	R	E	D	R
D	L	U	I	B	W	P	V	X	E
S	V	L	O	V	I	N	G	Z	A
Q	R	I	Y	L	Z	H	R	U	D
P	A	T	I	E	N	C	E	Q	Y
G	I	K	X	P	D	S	N	L	W
J	J	H	S	B	Z	V	E	N	P
H	M	O	D	N	H	C	R	B	E
K	A	F	Y	C	S	M	G	F	R
T	E	Q	H	A	P	P	Y	M	T

Now take a moment to reflect on how you feel about those words. Do they describe your current feelings? Actions? Thoughts? Think deeply before continuing on the workbook.

_____
_____
_____
_____
_____
_____
_____
_____
_____
_____
_____
_____
_____
_____
_____
_____
_____
_____
_____
_____
_____
_____
_____
_____
_____
_____
_____

"White people think it isn't happening because it isn't happening to them."

--Jane Elliot

Overcoming White Fragility with Humility

Before you begin this section on white fragility, define the term below.

White fragility is "discomfort and defensiveness on the part of a white person when confronted by information about racial inequality and injustice."[11] It is the result of a failure to acknowledge white-centering. White people who refuse to believe racism is real act from pride and ego, turning themselves into the victims.

---

[11] "White Fragility." https://www.lexico.com/en/definition/white_fragility

Overcoming white fragility is an opportunity for growth. When race comes up, notice what you feel in your body. Do you get nervous, uneasy, or defensive? Ask yourself why that is. Ask yourself if you're willing to listen. Ask yourself if you're willing to give credence to what people are saying, even if their experience has been different from yours. Ask yourself the motives of the other people in the conversation.

Understand that if what someone is saying about their experience with your race doesn't apply directly to you, you can choose to not take it personally.

For example, if someone says, "White people owned slaves," they're not saying you owned them personally, but you do still benefit from those actions today while Black people still suffer the residual consequences.

Now, let me be clear: You do NOT have to stand around and take anybody's abuse. If someone is calling you names, demeaning you, and is unwilling to hear you no matter how earnestly you're trying, they could just have an axe to grind, and you don't owe that behavior your attention.

Being an ally means reading between the lines and applying a vast amount of wisdom to the nuances of the situations at hand.

What does all this have to do with white fragility?

When you learn the history and understand the injustices around you, that information has the potential to shake everything you've grown to believe about your country. As Americans, we have been taught pithy statements about how people are dying to get here, we have more freedoms than anybody else, and we are the only ones who stand for liberty and justice for all.

And then your eyes open.

You learn that we have more people in prison than any other country in world history, and while Black people make up 13% of the population, they make up nearly 40% of the prison population.

[12] Here are more realities about Black people in the USA:
- Black people are often denied loan opportunities, despite high credit scores.
- Black people get poorer health care and have worse health outcomes than white counterparts, despite socioeconomic status.
- The school-to-prison pipeline prepares many Black students for prison instead of higher education.

These realities are just a few of many, many more hard-to-swallow pills, but you have a choice: you defend it, ignore it, or work to change it.

Are these statistics something you were aware of? If not, how do they make you feel? What are some actions you can take to help bring awareness or improve these statistics?

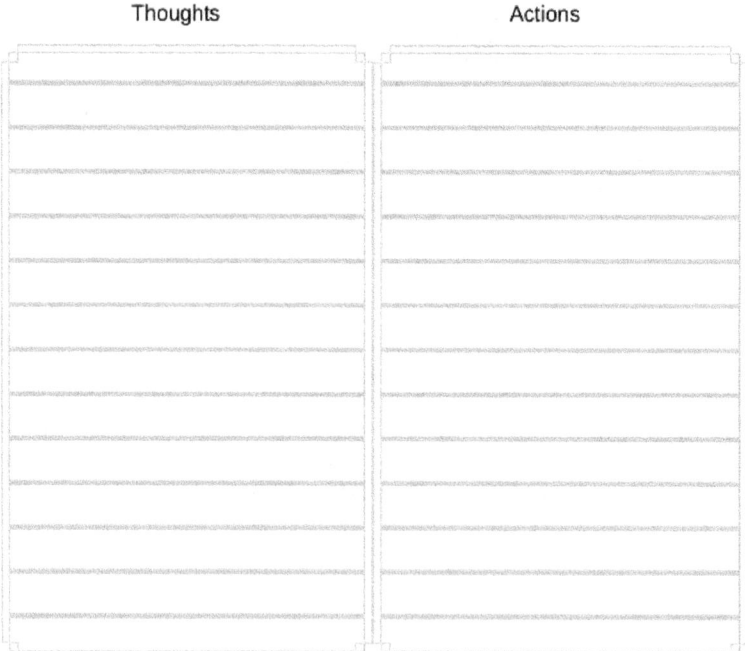

Understanding Black America

Thoughts	Actions

---

[12]Pariona, Amber. https://www.worldatlas.com/articles/incarceration-rates-by-race-ethnicity-and-gender-in-the-u-s.html

Jane Elliot, long-time anti-racist advocate and ally, forces her listeners into honest self-examination.

She tells the bare truth about what America is and what it represents and pushes her audiences to ponder the truth of our society, considering how it has affected them directly and indirectly. Elliot knows that before any meaningful progress can take place, white fragility has to go.

You can let the truth make you bitter, or you can let it make you better, and if it makes you better, it makes your country better. Truth is so powerful, it can transform this country into finally representing what we've been told all this time it already does.

Because you have a measure of humility, you are working through this book. However, humility isn't easy.

As you dismantle beliefs, you will want to push against some of what you read or learn. You must intentionally renew your sense of humility while going through this process, otherwise, you may be tempted to throw in the towel to preserve your pride. If that happens, no one wins.

It takes humility to admit when you're wrong, even if you were just doing what you were taught. This quality isn't only important for a social movement, it's important for personal growth, as well. Be humble when dismantling problematic beliefs, and be humble when rebuilding beliefs based on new, more complete information.

ALLY BINGO

Work through my Allyship workbook!	Read books by BIPOC authors	Think critically about the media I consume	Donate my time, talent, money, etc. to an org focused on POC liberation	Amplify BIPOC voices
Check in on BIPOC friends, family, and colleagues	Not get caught up in guilt	Doing internal reflection to better myself	VOTE for diverse candidates that match your values	Make representation a priority in my home
Listen to the BIPOC commnity when they speak	Show up to support at local events	Challenge my friends, family, and colleagues real time	Learn from my mistakes and continue forward	Welcome discomfort
Research when I have questions	Avoid performative Allyship!	Lend my voice to the BIPOC community	Relearn my countries history	Offer mentorship in professional settings when appropriate
Support BIPOC businesses	Not expect BIPOC friends, family, or colleagues to do the work for me	Have difficult conversations	Do not make myself the center of BIPOC conversations	Stay engaged in doing the work

HOW TO PLAY

Cross off or color in the bingo card **with the aspects of allyship you have already started.**

You complete the card by **blacking out the board.** Once you have blacked out the board, use the empty one underneath this one to create your own to continue your journey.

ALLY BINGO

HOW TO PLAY — Use this empty bingo board to create your next Allyship goals on your journey.

Where the Rubber Meets the Road

Once we understand the idea of anti-racism, what do we do with it?

We move from theoretical idealism to mental, physical, and emotional work.

Will we ever root out racism with such success that we one day won't have to see it again? No.

Can we make sure we don't contribute to it, that anybody watching doesn't learn mistreatment of others from us, and racists know their views won't be tolerated when we're around? Yep.

Responsibility

As people have become more open to learning about the Black experience in the United States, the responsibility to teach that history has fallen on the shoulders of Black people. Similarly, we see a rise of openness to histories of other POC. If we want to understand our country's history as holistically as possible, all BIPOC experiences are important to understand. However, since I identify as a Black woman, I'll be using the Black experience in this section, as it's the only one I can speak to.

It seems logical that if you want to know something and you have a living resource available, you should go straight to that source for your information, but this line of thinking requires a bit of nuance and empathy.

Black people, as a whole, are tired of the work and baggage that accompany navigating life in this country in our skin tones, and most of us aren't excitedly awaiting the opportunity to share our trauma with people who could work to get the same information from already-established, reputable sources. When you ask about our experiences, make sure you've done some work on your own to ensure you are in the headspace to listen, reflect, and understand our positions.

As an ally, the onus is on you to learn and to respect a POC when they don't feel like educating you. We are exasperated, mentally, spiritually, and emotionally, and we don't always know when someone is genuine in their quest for knowledge or when they're trying to bait us.

Part of educating yourself is knowing that the Black community has often been burned by members of the white community's misuse of the information we give them.

There is a lack of trust between the two communities, and one way you can help build trust is to do the intellectual work beforehand so we see you as a partner, not as a student.

Think about it:

1. How much time have you invested in the past year learning about the racist roots of the United States and how past actions have direct consequences on marginalized people today?

_____
_____
_____
_____
_____
_____
_____
_____
_____
_____
_____
_____

2. How many of the resources you used to gain this knowledge were written by POC?

_____
_____
_____
_____
_____
_____
_____
_____
_____
_____
_____
_____

3. List three things you have learned during such studies. If you haven't engaged in any study like this, why not?

4. Do you find it increasingly easier or increasingly more difficult to have conversations about race? Why?

The Work

Now that we've established a foundation, let's talk about the work.

The work never ends. When people accuse others of "playing the race card", what they fail to see is when you're not part of the racial majority in your country, almost everything--if not everything--really is about race. So much of our history is derived from race that it touches everything we do.

The effects of racism range from who gets to vote without obstacles to who can get a business loan. They determine whether you can hang out in a coffee shop until your friend arrives without being arrested or not. The threat hangs out in the most obvious places and the most inconspicuous ones. Since we've seen it everywhere, we expect to see it anywhere.

Start to tune your senses to the experiences of the marginalized. With new eyes, pay attention to the racism around you that has always been there.

Until you make the conscious effort to really *see*, racism remains theoretical, but that's not where it ends.

Even though you may see the signs around you, you might want to revert to a feeling of safety, a feeling that things are okay as they are, or that things aren't that bad because they're better than they were during the days of Jim Crow or slavery. It takes a daily commitment to not sink back into safety.

Just remember, the people you are supporting don't have the option to sink back. Many of the spaces that are safe for you are places of contention for us, and while outward expressions have changed, the date on the calendar hasn't changed mindsets; the election of Donald Trump and the continuous fight for his return prove that.

It is compulsory to be honest with yourself and ask if your skin tone has protected you, which is why things that may seem normal to you are off-limits to somebody else.

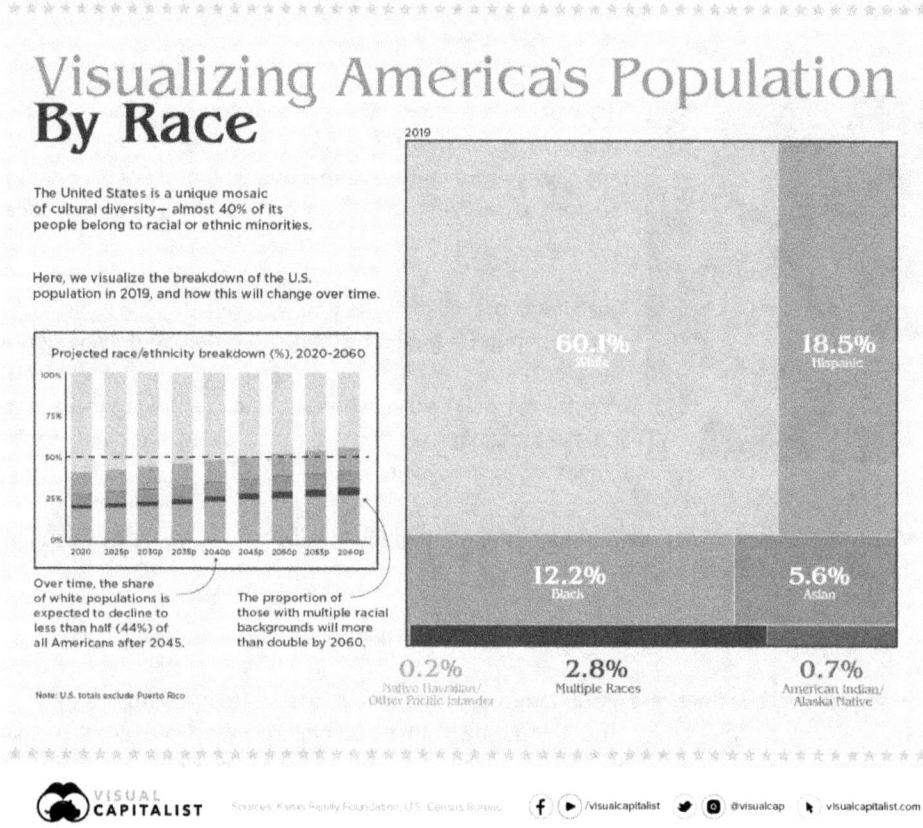

[13]Ghosh, Iman. https://www.visualcapitalist.com/visualizing-u-s-population-by-race/

Consider:

1. Has Segregation 2.0 put you at tables and in rooms that others, despite their achievements and qualifications, can't get into or only get into because someone is trying to meet a diversity quota?

_____
_____
_____
_____
_____
_____
_____
_____
_____
_____
_____
_____
_____

2. Look up the harm diversity quotas can cause and list your findings here.

3. What freedoms and privileges are afforded you as you go through everyday life that others may not enjoy?

Take a moment to think about things you do without a thought that Black people cannot do simply because of their skin.

Over the past five years, the issue of police brutality has finally been placed front and center, so we'll use that as an example.

Ask a white friend if they have ever backtalked a cop. If they have, ask for details about that experience. Is it something they thought about doing before it happened, or was it just second nature? When it happened, what were their thoughts immediately afterward? How did the officer react?

After that discussion, engage a Black friend in the same conversation and see if you even make it to the second question.

Part 3:

Adopt Your Personal Allyship Plan

You have learned so much. What are you going to do with your newfound knowledge? How are you going to grow because of it?

It's time to formulate a game plan. Go back through this workbook and remind yourself of all the work you've done. Start at the beginning with the first activity and explore your growth throughout the pages.

Take a moment to reflect and refocus on your goals.

_____
_____
_____
_____
_____
_____
_____
_____
_____
_____
_____
_____
_____
_____
_____
_____
_____
_____
_____
_____
_____
_____
_____
_____
_____
_____

In this final section, you will map out practical actionable steps. Remember that allyship is a journey, so when you complete the steps in your game plan, reformulate the plan and keep pushing.

There is always more to do. We have hundreds of years of systemic injustice to battle.

Ready?

1. Take a few moments to define your why. What has moved you towards this place of allyship? List up to four reasons for embarking on this journey and any accompanying thoughts.

My Whys

My Visual Allyship Journey

Draw or paste images that paint your Allyship Story

My initial thoughts and or fears about racism, discrimination and allyship	Things I've learned about racism, discrimination and allyship

When allyship doesn't happen these kinds of things can happen	My personal contributions are

2. What does your privilege give you access to? What resources (people, materials, skills, or time) could you utilize for organizations, communities, or individuals to make positive change towards equality in your community? List various ways you could see this playing out.

My Resources	Potential Uses

3. List some specific changes that you'd like to see because of your allyship.

The three tables above, coupled with the list of community organizations you made at the beginning of this workbook, comprise your Allyship Game Plan.
Here's your call to action.

If you did not already call one of those organizations who are working to improve the community where or near where you live, do it today. Once you speak with their representative, write about the conversation(s) and the work you can do immediately. It doesn't matter how big or small the step is--if it's with the right mindset and attitude, it's a step in the right direction.

The conversation:

_____
_____
_____
_____
_____
_____
_____
_____
_____
_____
_____
_____
_____
_____
_____
_____
_____
_____
_____
_____
_____
_____
_____
_____
_____
_____
_____
_____

Remember, change isn't fast.

The work you do now will set a strong foundation so others who come behind you will be able to continue it. You don't have to be another Jane Elliot to be effective--you just need to make sure your motives are pure and your actions are useful.

Allyship is about unity.

If you understand unity in action, you're on the right track.

"Equality is the soul of liberty. There is, in fact, no liberty without it."

--Frances Wright

ACKNOWLEDGEMENTS

I couldn't have done this without the help of two very important contributors; my dearest friend and colleague Whitney Marsh, and my editor and advisor Jasmine Cochran.

Having Jasmine's guidance and perspective throughout this process has been both rewarding and comforting.

Whitney has acted as a doula in the birth of this work. Her ability to grasp the vision of others and deliver it perfectly, even in the ninth hour, always blows me away.

Doing this during what feels like a never ending pandemic presented a very unique set of nuances and complexities. As three Black women we were all dealing with what many would call *stressful post pandemic life*. For Black women this can feel as though we should be debilitated, but life has to go on. Together, we did what Black women do, and for that I am beyond grateful.

Jasmine Cochran
Content Editor
Jasmine Cochran is CEO of Jasmine Cochran Consulting and founder of *History Confronted*, a database of BIPOC accomplishments. She's consulted with educators worldwide to diversify curricula. In 2020, Jasmine served as an inaugural Democrats Abroad Black Global Caucus Poet Laureate. Find her at www.jasminecochran.com

Whitney Marsh
Project Manager & Curriculum Builder
Whitney Marsh is a Project Manager and Curriculum Builder. She has a masters in Ethnic Studies which gave her the passion for DEI that she has. She consults with companies of all sizes on developing their DEI content. Contact her at whitney.marsh@yumyummorale.com and find her at
https://www.linkedin.com/in/whitney-marsh/

Resources

"Discrimination." *Lexico*. 2021. https://www.lexico.com/en/definition/discrimination

Foster, Alyssa. "Speaks Volumes Anti Racism Activist & Educator Jane Elliot Speaks To White Citizens On Receiving." *YouTube*. 2016. https://www.youtube.com/watch?v=xUIqTNwm-mk

Ghosh, Iman. "Visualizing the U.S. Population by Race." *Visual Capitalist*. 2020. https://www.visualcapitalist.com/visualizing-u-s-population-by-race/

Gonzalez, Juan Carlos. "The ordinary-ness of institutional racism: the effect of history and law in the segregation and integration of Latinas/os in schools." *American Educational History Journal*, vol. 34, no. 1-2, annual 2007, pp. 331+. *Gale Academic OneFile*, link.gale.com/apps/doc/A252849366/AONE?u=anon~2ad6102a&sid=googleScholar&xid=d7657ee7. Accessed 4 Dec. 2021.

Koppelman, Andrew. "What is systemic racism, anyway?" *USA Today*. 2020. https://www.usatoday.com/story/opinion/2020/09/23/systemic-racism-how-really-define-column/5845788002/

Lu, Denise, et. al. "Faces of Power: 80% Are White, Even as U.S. Becomes More Diverse." *The New York Times*. 2020. https://www.nytimes.com/interactive/2020/09/09/us/powerful-people-race-us.html

Pariona, Amber. "US Prison Population By Race." *World Atlas*. 2019. https://www.worldatlas.com/articles/incarceration-rates-by-race-ethnicity-and-gender-in-the-u-s.html

"Racism." *Dictionary.com*. 2021. https://www.dictionary.com/browse/racism

Romanelli, Assael, Ph.D." Core Beliefs: The Hammer We Hold in Our Hand." *Psychology Today*. 2020. https://www.psychologytoday.com/us/blog/the-other-side-relationships/202001/core-beliefs-the-hammer-we-hold-in-our-hand#:~:text=These%20beliefs%20are%20called%20core%20beliefs%20and%20they,they%20cannot%20be%20disproved%20because%20they%20are%20all-encompassing.

Saad, Layla F., and Robin DiAngelo. *Me and White Supremacy: Combat Racism, Change the World, and Become a Good Ancestor*. Thorndike Press, a Part of Gale, a Cengage Company, 2020.

"Stand Your Ground and Castle Doctrine Laws." *Bill of Rights Institute*. https://billofrightsinstitute.org/e-lessons/stand-your-ground-and-castle-doctrine-laws-elesson

"White Fragility." *Lexico.com*. 2021. https://www.lexico.com/en/definition/white_fragility

Zinn, Howard. *A People's History of the United States*. Harper, 2017. Chapters 2&3.

www.ingramcontent.com/pod-product-compliance
Lightning Source LLC
Chambersburg PA
CBHW081405070526
44583CB00020B/2682